THE HERO IN YOU

ELLIS PAUL   Pictures by ANGELA PADRÓN

Albert Whitman & Company
Chicago, Illinois

To my little heroines, Ella and Sofi—EP

For Alonzo, my little hero—AP

Library of Congress Cataloging-in-Publication Data

Paul, Ellis.
The hero in you / by Ellis Paul ; illustrations by Angela Padron.
pages cm
Summary: "A collection of songs celebrating the accomplishments of thirteen heroes from United States history,
including Nellie Bly, Chief Joseph, and Ben Franklin.
The final song celebrates the potential hero in each of us"—Provided by publisher.
1. Children's songs, English—United States—Texts. 2. Heroes—Songs and music.
[1. Heroes—Songs and music. 2. Individuality—Songs and music. 3. Biography—Songs and music. 4. Songs.]
I. Padrón, Angela, illustrator. II. Title.
PZ8.3.P27367He 2014
782.42—dc23
2014000630

Published in 2014 by Albert Whitman & Company
ISBN 978-0-8075-3238-6 (hardcover)
ISBN 978-0-8075-3239-3 (hardcover)

The design is by Nick Tiemersma.

For more information about Albert Whitman & Company,
visit our web site at www.albertwhitman.com.

I wrote this music—and now this book—to remind parents and children about some of the truly amazing people this country has produced.

As we've been confronted by war, terrorism, class struggles, and political divides, I worry that our perception of ourselves has become more about our challenges than our victories. So I set out to write music that says, "this is who we really are." I hope it will inspire kids to reach for the better parts of themselves. A nation is only as good as its heroes, and we truly need more.

If you're a kid reading this: remember that at one time Abraham Lincoln, Jackie Robinson, and the Beatles were kids too. They were dreamers, writers, painters, science geeks, and athletes. A lot of the work they did as grown-ups had roots in the dreams they had as kids. So keep dreaming! Dream out loud! Start now!

—Ellis Paul

"I have never written a word that did not come from my heart. I never shall."
—Nellie Bly

Nellie Bly

Nellie Bly, Nellie Bly
The world could be yours if you try, if you try

Nellie Bly was just a girl, born into a world
 where little girls barely mattered
  Even women couldn't vote
   Their jobs just left them broke
   Sewing clothes and stirring batter

  Nellie didn't think it was right
  She took up a pen to fight for women's rights
  And she told the whole world
  what it's all about

  Nellie Bly, she was sly, she was like a private eye
  She went undercover into a women's mental ward
  Her pen was like a sword
   She played sick to be among the others

  The patients weren't being treated right
  She stayed there ten long days and nights
  Then she told the whole world
  what it's all about!

  Nellie Bly was just a girl in a race around the world
  Taking trains and ships on steam power
  She sailed the China sea with her pet monkey
  Meeting kings and getting flowers

  Arabia, Hong Kong, Singapore
  In seventy-two days she was on American shores
  Telling the whole…wide…world
what it's all about!

Nellie Bly completed a trip around the world in seventy-two days—a new world record at the time!

Nellie Bly was one of the first female journalists to go undercover to research a story.

One of her most famous stories helped lead to better conditions at hospitals.

Nellie Bly was the pen name for Elizabeth Jane Cochrane.

TODAY'S NEWS 5¢

TODAY'S NEWS 5¢

5¢

AUGUSTUS JACKSON

He did not invent ice cream but invented a way to make it last long enough to be shipped and sold.

He is known as the "father of ice cream."

Strawberry, chocolate, vanilla ice cream
Old Augustus Jackson's got an ice cream machine
He puts in a little flavor, sugar, and ice
Then he mixes it with salt and cream
It tastes real nice

Augustus Jackson was a free black man
A chef at the White House for the Madisons
He came to Philadelphia when they set him free
He started making ice cream on Goodwater Street
And the people came
Calling out his flavors by name

Augustus Jackson invented a way
to make his ice cream last for days and days
He built his empire up from the ground
by shipping ice cream in tins all over town
No matter what flavor you are
you can fill up a spoon at Jackson's ice cream bar

Augustus Jackson was once a cook at the White House for President James Madison.

WOODY GUTHRIE

Woody's jumping on a train
In a boxcar in the rain
Under one big sky
Wipes the dust out of his eye

He's out here seeking truth
His guitar's cutting loose
A Dustbowl stray
On the ribbon of highway

He's an Okie locomotive rider
Singing, thinking, freedom fighter
Sketching lyric pictures of this land

He's a poet, picker, writer, painter
Mystic, prophet, entertainer
Woody Guthrie, Working Man!

Under California skies, Okies were broken
Or just getting by
In the orchards 'round their radio
There's a voice there that's giving them hope

He wrote songs out on Coney Isle
that made his children and Pete Seeger smile
Songs for workers and the Grand Coulee Dam
For soldiers of war and for old Uncle Sam

He was born in the old Dust Bowl
A red dirt cowboy with a childlike soul
From New York to the Rio Grande
He kept on singing all the way to California
"This land is your land"

"I DON'T WANT THE KIDS TO BE GROWN-UP. I WANT TO SEE THE GROWN FOLKS BE KIDS."—WOODY GUTHRIE

CHIEF JOSEPH

I am a child of the Wallowa Valley
    in the wilds of Oregon
I am "Thunder Rolling Down the Mountain"
I was born a chief's son
The Nez Perce were my people
Looking Glass was my friend
And we lived our lives in the western hills
till the white man camp closing in
closing in…

From where the sun now stands
I will fight no more forever
And we will all remain together
From where the sun now stands

10,000 years the land was ours
if any can own the land
We believe no trees, no wind, no earth
are the property of man
General Howard, he came to find us
His government would not agree
So the land was claimed by the white man
and my people had to flee
my people had to flee

In the Bear Paw Mountains
just miles from freedom's hand
We sold our homes, we sold our bones
and surrendered all our land
What is the price of freedom?
What is the pay in grief?
And what do we surrender
    to live our lives in peace
live our lives in peace?

"In nature, nothing exists alone." -Rachel Carson

RACHEL CARSON

Rachel went a'walkin' in the woods at twilight
Talking to the animals, listening to the trees
She heard the beauty in the whistling songbird
The rustling of the hickory, the buzzing of the bees

She wandered, wondering, what could she bring
to give a voice to the silence of the spring

One day came the big bulldozers
The planes dropping chemicals
People cutting trees
Rachel saw the bald eagle suffering
high up in the canopy
to the edge of the sea

And, oh, they're tearing the big trees down
They're covering the crops with a cloud of spray
And the bulldozers and the high-rises from town
come so close you can't hear the forest sounds

Rachel wrote a book on an old typewriter
about the poison in the atmosphere
and in the air we breathe
She told the truth and the world started listening
She was talking for the animals
Speaking for the trees.

Carson's writing helped change laws about the use of pesticides that harm wildlife.

Because of Rachel's writing, the dangerous pesticide DDT was banned.

She worked for the U.S. Bureau of Fisheries and the U.S. Fish and Wildlife Service.

Carson gave a voice to animals and plants that were suffering from the effects of pollution.

MORE THAN 26,000 PEOPLE CAME TO SEE JACKIE ROBINSON'S FIRST TIME PLAYING FOR THE DODGERS.

JACKIE ROBINSON ALSO PLAYED FOOTBALL, BASKETBALL, AND TRACK. HE WAS ONE OF THE BEST LONG JUMPERS IN THE WORLD!

"A LIFE IS NOT IMPORTANT EXCEPT IN THE IMPACT IT HAS ON OTHER LIVES."
-JACKIE ROBINSON

ROBINSON JOINED THE BROOKLYN DODGERS IN 1947.

JACKIE ROBINSON WAS THE FIRST AFRICAN AMERICAN TO PLAY MAJOR LEAGUE BASEBALL.

JACKIE ROBINSON

Jackie Robinson was a man who swung a bat
And because he was so good at it
he became much more than that
He was the first man of color in the game
He rose from the Negro Leagues into fame
Into a world that was begging for change
In the dug out they gave him a shout out
They're calling his name

Jackie Robinson
Jackie Robinson
Jackie Robinson
You've changed the way
we play the game!

Baseball, football, basketball,
long jump, and track
He was a world-class athlete
No game was gonna hold him back
Oh, he was called up
to rise above all the shame
The slurs and the threats that he overcame
His courage belongs in the hall of fame
In the dugout
They gave him a shout out
They're calling his name

ALBERT EINSTEIN

Einstein, your mind was so ahead of its time
Your math was so divine
It showed how the world was beautiful

But your teacher confessed
You'd never be a success
You put her theory to the test
When you showed how the world was beautiful

E=mc2
Energy is equal to mass times the speed of light
Squared
You never combed your hair
Sometimes the smallest star is the brightest sight
(Were you too busy thinking to make it look right?)

You showed light bent
Whenever gravity was present
And no matter where you went
The camera flashed and you were beautiful

World war knocking at your door
What is all this hatred for?
You fought for peace
Till the fighting ceased
As they closed their eyes
And then demanded more
You opened the door

Space flight, TV
These things would just never be
Without you, Albert, in our history
You showed that the world was beautiful

$$G\mu\nu = 8\pi T\mu\nu$$

$$E_k = \frac{1}{2}mv^2$$

ALBERT
EINSTEIN'S
THEORIES
HELPED
CREATE
NUCLEAR
POWER.

"I knew someone had to take the
first step and I made up my mind
not to move." —Rosa Parks

Rosa Parks

The wheels on the bus, they go round and round...
Back in 1955 in Montgomery on a city street
There's a bus on a corner with police cars
and a woman sitting down in her seat

You know what's right
You know what's wrong
The signs are coming down
It's been going on too long

You know what's wrong
You know what's right
Rosa's gonna fight
It's been going on too long

Rosa was arrested 'cause a white man
asked for her seat and she wouldn't give it up
Martin Luther King helped form a boycott
No blacks would ride the bus until it stopped

Sometimes the best way
To fight for a better day
Is sitting down
Not fighting!
Sitting down, make it right and
Sit down to stand up
Sit down to stand up
Sit down to stand up
For your rights!

You don't need no violence to set it right
Make a change, change, change

Rosa brought change and a movement came
Where people fought for their civil rights
In school, in work, and in traveling
It should be equal if you're black or white

Rosa Parks was arrested for refusing to give up her seat for a white passenger.

Rosa inspired black residents of Montgomery to boycott the buses until the laws were changed.

Her act of civil disobedience was one of the key moments of the Civil Rights Movement.

Old Ben Franklin, I think we should thank him
Was a poet and a diplomat
He put a key out on a kite
Till he saw the lightnin' strike
But what's shocking is
He did way more than that

He put bifocals on our nose
He made a better wood stove
Made lightning rods for all the homes in Philly
He helped the Declaration pass
He made music out of glass
Fought the British
And said lots of things that were silly

Old Ben Franklin, I think we should thank him
He was the world's most industrious guy
He said, "Early to bed, early to rise,
makes a man healthy, wealthy,
and wise"

He was a fireman, a patriot,
He was a kite flyer
He was a printer, he was a writer
He was Postmaster General, an ambassador
He was a musician, a revolutionary
A humorist, he was a philosopher

"He that is good for making excuses,
is seldom good for anything else"
"An investment in knowledge pays the best interest"
"Fish and guests go bad after three days"
"A man wrapped up in himself makes a very small bundle"

Say, hey, Benny, they didn't put you on the penny
Though you wrote this with your mighty quill
You said, "A penny saved is a penny earned"
So they put you on the hundred dollar bill
That's lots of pennies!

Mr. Tee Tot

Mr. Tee Tot sat down on the boulevard
With his guitar and his old creaking chair
And Hank sat at his feet, sipping summer tea so sweet

Mr. Tee Tot, talk awhile
Sing a song and make me smile
Mr. Tee Tot, won't you talk awhile

He said, "Son, I once had a catfish on a fishing pole
And he fought me for four nights and four days
Till the river met the sea, then that catfish says to me,
'I fought you for four nights, four days
Brought you the moon and this beautiful bay
Now, unhook me, mister! Set me free!'"

Mr. Tee Tot played an F chord minor seven
And he sang just like a lion loose from a cage
He said, "'Catfish, can't you see, I've got to feed my family...'
So I ate him. I filleted him. Buttered him so much I bathed him.
It took me four long days to catch him, but only four hours to eat."

He said, "Son, they're gonna tell you it's all about the journey
And not the destination when you get there.
But I'll say when you do, the best part does come true.
If you share, you've gotta share, you've gotta share."

Tee Tot was a popular street musician in Alabama.

There are no known photos of Tee Tot.

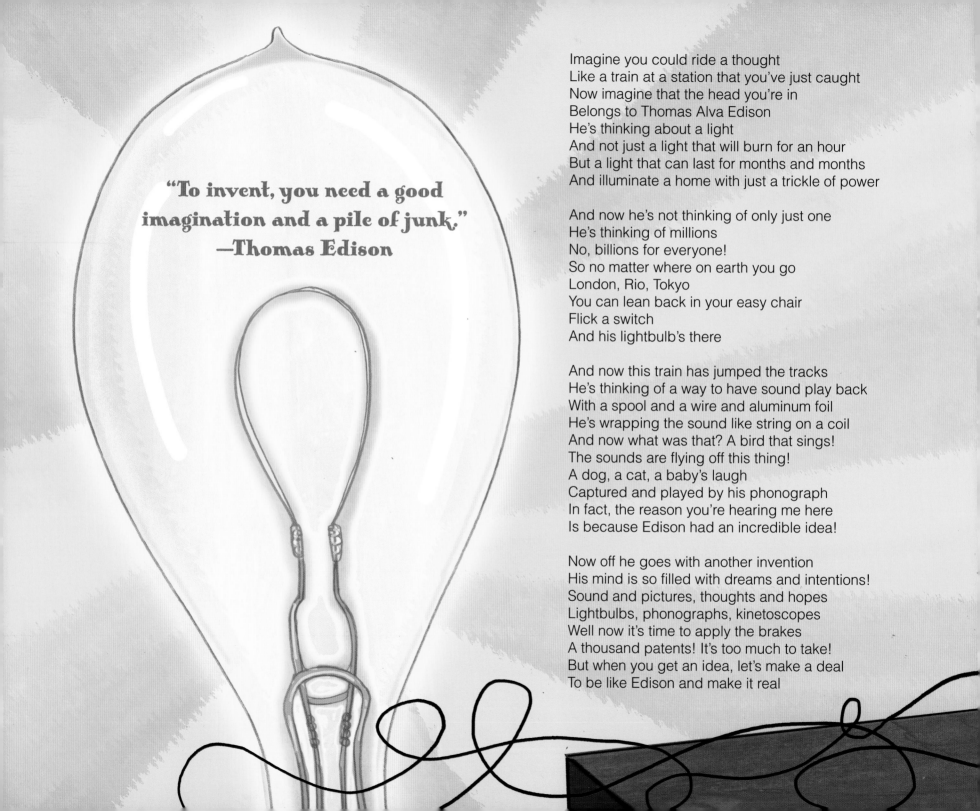

"To invent, you need a good imagination and a pile of junk."
—Thomas Edison

Imagine you could ride a thought
Like a train at a station that you've just caught
Now imagine that the head you're in
Belongs to Thomas Alva Edison
He's thinking about a light
And not just a light that will burn for an hour
But a light that can last for months and months
And illuminate a home with just a trickle of power

And now he's not thinking of only just one
He's thinking of millions
No, billions for everyone!
So no matter where on earth you go
London, Rio, Tokyo
You can lean back in your easy chair
Flick a switch
And his lightbulb's there

And now this train has jumped the tracks
He's thinking of a way to have sound play back
With a spool and a wire and aluminum foil
He's wrapping the sound like string on a coil
And now what was that? A bird that sings!
The sounds are flying off this thing!
A dog, a cat, a baby's laugh
Captured and played by his phonograph
In fact, the reason you're hearing me here
Is because Edison had an incredible idea!

Now off he goes with another invention
His mind is so filled with dreams and intentions!
Sound and pictures, thoughts and hopes
Lightbulbs, phonographs, kinetoscopes
Well now it's time to apply the brakes
A thousand patents! It's too much to take!
But when you get an idea, let's make a deal
To be like Edison and make it real

THOMAS EDISON

He helped figure out how to deliver electricity for streetlights and to private homes.

Edison improved the design of the lightbulb so it could be used in every home.

He had over one thousand patents!

She was a smart girl, young girl
Loved to dance
In fact she did it every time she got the chance
She learned the moves, like a list of rules
Studied ballet when she went to school
She could pirouette, balance
She could jump and spin and battement glissé
But her soul felt lost
Heart was locked
Like she was dancing inside of someone else's box
So she arched her back, fell to the floor
'Cause that's what expressed the emotion more
Sometime you gotta draw outside of the lines
To color the dance that's inside your mind

You've gotta dance like Martha
Dance like Martha
Dance like Martha
Dance...

Many of her dances were influenced by the world events that were happening around her, like wars and the Great Depression.

Martha Graham

She danced for over seventy years!

Graham was the first dancer to perform at the White House.

And then the day came, Martha started a school
  She taught the dancers how to dance beyond the rules
    World War II, the Great Depression
    All could play a part in her imagination
    All the costumes and all the props
    Were just another way to make the audience's heart stop

      These actors, dancers were part of a play
        And Martha danced so you could feel the day
        All the heartache, all the joy
        Expressed in the moves of these girls and boys
        If you could dance your fear, would you take the chance?
        'Cause that's how Martha chose to dance

"You are unique, and if that is not fulfilled, then something has been lost." —Martha Graham

"I decided that if I could paint that flower in a huge scale, you could not ignore its beauty." —Georgia O'Keeffe

Georgia O'Keeffe

In 1946, the Museum of Modern Art in New York opened a major exhibition of her art—the first for a woman artist there.

She was inspired by the nature that surrounded her, especially in New Mexico.

Georgia O'Keeffe saw beauty where others could not—in addition to flowers, she painted animal skulls!

No one can see the world through your eyes
No one can see this world through your eyes

Look at the poppy fields and the desert sky
Let your paintbrush answer
All of the whats and whys

See the things that others
Just pass on by
Go put your paint to canvas
Make the mountains rise

Paint your boldest color
Your brightest idea
The smallest passing moment
In your longest passing year

The petals of a flower
Veins dancing 'cross a leaf
Go live your dream
Georgia O'Keeffe

The way you see the world
In the power of a flower
The lights of New York City
The sky in the day's last hour

No one can see the world through your eyes
No one can see this world through your eyes
Unless you paint it, unless you write it
Unless you dance it, and take a chance on it

THE HERO IN YOU

Everybody's got a story
of all their troubles, all their glories
Tell me yours, you cannot bore me
I love to listen to you

All your bumps and all your scratches
All your holes and all your patches—
It's you! It's true! You have no matches
There's a hero in you

You can make the hero you are
with your brains, your aim,
and your battle scars

Everybody's got a tale
of how they chased a great white whale
Some succeeded and some just failed
But trying is what you've got to do
'Cause in the trying you feel you're flying
The whole wide world is beneath you lying
It's you! It's true! There's no denying
There's a hero in you.

So use your brain and do some thinking
You could be the next Abe Lincoln
Use your muscle, try to hustle
You could be Muhammad Ali
Use your toes and dance on pumpkins
You could be Isadora Duncan
It's you, it's true! I hope it sunk in
There's a hero in you.

Nellie Bly

(1864–1922) was one of the first female investigative journalists. Her work as an undercover reporter broke new ground. She disguised herself as a patient to expose the terrible conditions at an asylum, and her story led to positive changes and better conditions at hospitals.

AUGUSTUS JACKSON

(1808–1852) was a freed slave who changed the way ice cream was sold. Formerly a cook at the White House, Jackson became an ice-cream maker in Philadelphia. He invented a way to make ice cream last long enough to be shipped and sold. He was one of the most successful African American businessmen of his time.

WOODY GUTHRIE

(1912–1967) was a folk musician and songwriter who wrote thousands of songs, including "This Land is Your Land." Many of his early songs are about the hard times people endured during the Great Depression, and throughout his career he wrote songs to address social problems in America.

CHIEF JOSEPH

(1840–1904) was the leader of the Wallowa band of the Nez Perce, a Native American tribe in the Northwest, during a time when the U.S. government was forcing them off their land. He is remembered as a pacifist but he was also a strong leader. Given the choice between fighting a war and surrendering for the sake of survival, he chose to protect his people.

Rachel Carson

(1907–1964) was a writer and scientist whose work made people more aware of the need for conservation. She wrote many books, including *Silent Spring*, which helped change laws about the use of pesticides. Her books also influenced new government offices dedicated to saving the environment.

JACKIE ROBINSON

(1919–1972) was the first African American to play Major League Baseball. Before then, black players could play only in the Negro Leagues. Robinson's career with the Brooklyn Dodgers was so successful that people began to question segregation in other areas of American life as well.

Albert Einstein

(1879–1955) was a brilliant physicist whose theories helped create nuclear power. He came to America from Germany in the years before WWII and warned President Roosevelt that the Nazis were trying to develop powerful atomic bombs. His ideas have helped us understand the universe.

Rosa Parks

(1913–2005) was arrested in Montgomery, Alabama, in 1955 for refusing to give up her bus seat for a white passenger. Her act of civil disobedience to protest racial discrimination was one of the key moments of the Civil Rights Movement. She helped make people see the injustice of racial segregation.

Ben Franklin

(1706–1790) was one of the founding fathers of the United States—he signed the Declaration of Independence—and was also a writer, inventor, publisher, politician, philosopher, statesman, and scientist. In all of his roles he wanted his work and inventions to be helpful to society as a whole.

Mr. Tee Tot aka

Rufus Payne (1884–1939) was a black musician in Alabama who gave music lessons to young Hank Williams. At the time, it was unusual—even dangerous—for a black man to mentor a white boy, but Tee Tot's instruction crossed racial boundaries and helped bring the blues to a larger audience.

Thomas Edison

(1847–1931) invented a great number of things that changed how we live, including the phonograph, the kinetoscope, and a wireless telegraph system. He also innovated industrial research, turning his New Jersey laboratory into a factory that worked constantly on creating new ideas.

Martha Graham

(1894–1991) was a dancer and choreographer who invented her own unique style of movement that still influences dancers today. She first learned how to dance ballet, but she went beyond the standard rules and turned dance into a new mode of self-expression.

Georgia O'Keeffe

(1887–1986) was a painter whose work helped introduce modern art to a wider audience. From painting small things like flowers on very large canvases to finding the beauty in unusual objects like animal skulls, O'Keeffe was interested in new ways of seeing nature and the world around her.

You are someone

special, and the story of your life is happening right now! It'll be a bumpy ride sometimes, but you'll learn a lot along the way. Maybe you'll invent something or write a book or become a leader. Or maybe you'll try something that's never been done before. How will you be a hero? It's up to you...